Text: Jordi Bonet i Armengol
Photographs: Miquel Badia, Tavisa and Photographics Archives Fisa-Escudo de Oro S.A.
Design, lay-out and printing, entirely created by the technical department of
EDITORIAL ESCUDO DE ORO S.A.
Rights of total or partial reproduction and translation reserved.
Copyright of this edition for photographs and text:
© EDITORIAL ESCUDO DE ORO S.A.

I.S.B.N. 84-378-2179-7
1st edition: January 2000

Printed by FISA-ESCUDO DE ORO S.A.
Palaudàries, 26 - 08004 Barcelona (Spain)
Legal Dep. B. 1559-2000

www.eoro.com
e-mail: editorial@eoro.com

TEMPLE
SAGRADA FAMÍLIA

Text:
Jordi Bonet i Armengol

THE HISTORICAL SETTING

The Sagrada Familia is the product of the circumstances stemming from its foundation and the unique drive of Antoni Gaudí, who devoted more than 40 years of his life as an architect to it.

The Catholic faith, which had a strong presence in the origins of Catalonia in the 10th century, again played a leading role in the nation's rebirth —the «Renaixença», or Renaissance— one thousand years later, when workers, farmers and intellectuals, amongst them the country-born priest and poet Jacint Verdaguer, restored their language to its rightful dignity.

The expansion of the city of Barcelona, with the industrial revolution and the impulse of the bourgeoisie, brought into being a powerful capital city where art flourished alongside trade and the economy. Catalonia once again opened up to the world, generously regaling it with all its finest and most personal achievements.

At a difficult moment for the Universal Church, a Barcelona bookseller, Josep Maria Bocabella, created the Association of Followers of Saint Joseph to give spiritual and material aid to the Holy See, proposing, moreover, to build a monumental church, dedicated to the Holy Family, to be surrounded by gardens, where respectable public leisure activities would be complemented by learning, education and spiritual contemplation.

Engraving of the city of Barcelona (late-19th century).

Western elevation and façade, designed by the architect Villar.

FOUNDING AND CORNERSTONE

A notarial document «bears witness that the Bishop of Barcelona, Josep Maria Urquinaona i Bidot, cloaked in the sacred ornaments and attended by the Bishop Elect of Vic, Dr Josep Morgades and other members of the clergy, in presence of the Captain General and other dignitaries, of Josep Maria Bocabella and Manuel de Dalmases, representing the Followers of Saint Joseph, of the architect F. P. De Villar, Elias Rogent, Director of the School of Architecture, and a large gathering of the faithful, solemnly proceeded to bless the land, placing the cornerstone of a Monumental Expiatory Church, to the greater glory of the Holy Family. To awaken from their slumbers the lukewarm heart, exalt the Faith, promote Charity, Invoke the Lord to have mercy on this country so that, encouraged by its Catholic roots, it will think, preach and practice the Virtues» (parchment text deposited in the cornerstone on 19 March 1882).

The walls of the crypt were about to be built when, due to disagreements with the Followers of Joseph, the architect and author of the project resigned. In around November 1883, a promising new architect, Antoni Gaudí i Cornet was commissioned to carry out the work.

Depiction of the ceremony of laying the first stone in the church.

Portrait of the founder, Josep Maria Bocabella, by Clapés.

GAUDÍ, ARCHITECT OF THE SAGRADA FAMILIA

Antoni Gaudí, born on 26 June 1852, was baptised in the Church of Sant Pere in Reus, then Catalonia's second city. The future architect's family were coppersmiths who struggled to give the young Gaudí an education. Reus was a dynamic, prosperous provincial city which, in the space of just a few years, produced such other men of great renown as Joan Prim, the general who became president of the Spanish government, and Marià Fortuny, a painter famous throughout Europe in the mid-19th century.

Having obtained his degree in architecture from the Barcelona School of Architecture in 1878, Gaudí soon distinguished himself in his chosen field of activity, receiving commissions from the man who would be his friend and patron, Eusebi Güell i Bacigalupi, as well as from the prestigious architect, Joan Martorell, who involved him in the Sagrada Familia project. He was also friendly with poet Joan Maragall, one of the great sponsors of the enterprise.

Gaudí attended the first reading of Mossen Jacint Verdaguer's poem «Canigó» (1883) in the cloisters of Elna Cathedral.

Antoni Gaudí i Cornet (1878).

DESCRIPTION

1.- A general idea

«In the Sagrada Familia, everything is providential» (Gaudí).

An important donation, received in around 1890, work on the church to be extended, and gave Gaudí the chance to develop his creative skills. The architect conceived the building as a pyramid-shaped volume which would stand out against the constructions of the city of Barcelona.

The church as a basilical ground plan in the form of a Latin cross, with nave and four aisles and transept with nave and two aisles. The interior of the church is 90 metres in length and 60 metres wide. The nave is 15 metres wide and the apse is delimited by seven chapels and two circular staircases, with ambulatory surrounding the presbytery. The building is surrounded by a cloister which links the three great fronts or façades giving entrance to it: on the east side, that of the Nativity, on the west side, that of the Passion and, on the south side, that of Glory. On either side of the apse are two buildings —the sacristies— which will in future be used for administration and services. A 170-metre high dome will rise over the centre of the transept, representing Jesus Christ, flanked by another four symbolising the Evangelists. Covering the apse will be another dome, dedicated to Our Lady.

Over the aisles and the head are tribunes which, with those of the apse, will accommodate a choir of 1,500 singers whose voices will join those of the faithful, bringing the total capacity of the Sagrada Familia to 15,000 people.

A great inner space of 900 square metres supported by four central columns will occupy the centre of the transept, which will have a maximum height of 60 metres. The apse is closed by an immense 75-metre high hyperboloid presided over by the figure of God the Creator accompanied by the angel hierarchies. The portals feature great porches embellished with iconographies of the Nativity, the Passion and the Glory, each crowned by four belltowers symbolising the twelve Apostles. Each column is dedicated to an apostle or to the Catalan and Spanish dioceses or those of the five continents. With the saints which have made them renowned in a synthesis of the universal nature of the Church, extending from East to West, as the first bishop of Tarragona, Saint Fructuoso prayed for at the moment of his martyrdom.

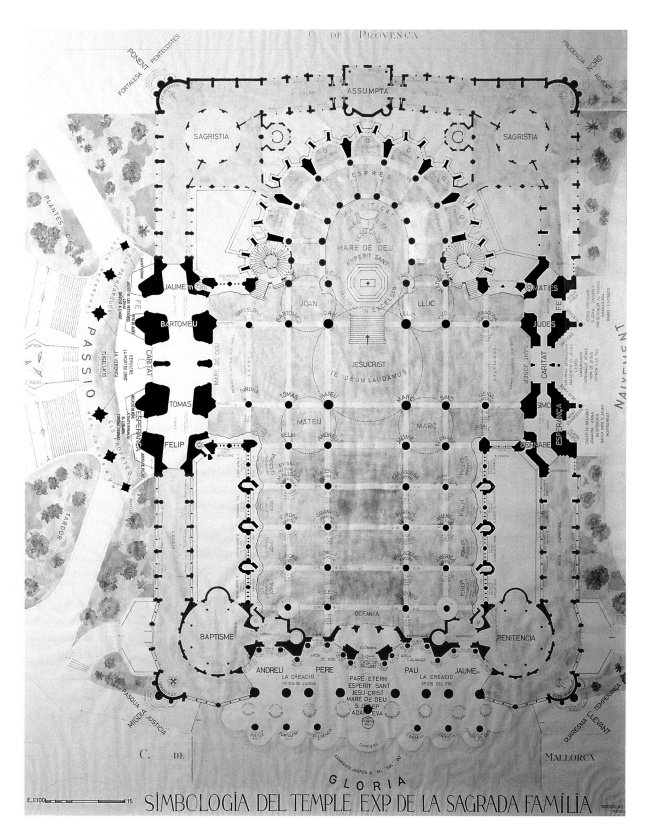

SIMBOLOGIA DEL TEMPLE EXP. DE LA SAGRADA FAMÍLIA

Overall plan of the church with its symbolism and dedication.

Overall idea of the church. Original drawing by Gaudí.

The church and the city.

2.- The crypt

Gaudí was commissioned to continue the work begun by Villar. He kept the ground plan, which had already been started, but modified the situation of the entrance staircases and raised the vault covering the entrance, its keystone embellished with a beautiful representation of the Annunciation, so that high windows could illuminate the space over the ambulatory which encircles it and separates it from the chapels. He also designed a large trench to surround the crypt, protecting it from damp and improving its lighting.

The chapels are dedicated to the members of the Holy Family of Jesus. In the centre is the Sacred Heart, flanked by the Immaculate Conception and Saint Joseph, along with Saint Joachim, Saint Anne, Saint Elizabeth and Saint Zacharias, Saint John the Baptist and Saint John the Evangelist. The Altar of Saint Joseph was inaugurated in 1885. This features neo-Gothic ornamentation, which Gaudí had studied in great detail.

At present, the crypt is where the life of the parish goes on. The high altar occupies the central area closest to the transept. On one side is the Holy Sacrament and on the other is the statue of Our Lady of Montserrat. A mosaic representing the vine and the grain is installed in the centre of the crypt. The chapels closing the ambulatory contain the tombs of the Bocabella and Dalmases families, as well as that of the architect, Antoni Gaudí.

Crypt keystone: the Annunciation.

Crypt: overall view.

Crypt. View of the ambulatory.

Crypt. In the background, the Chapel of Saint Joseph.

Chapel of Saint Joseph.

Altar of Our Lady of Montserrat.

Sacristy doorway.

Chapel of Carmen and the tomb of Antoni Gaudí.

3.- The apse

The apse, built between 1891 and 1895, is neo-Gothic in style, though it contains elements where Gaudí's personality clearly stands out. It consists of seven polygonal shaped chapels dedicated to the suffering and joy of Saint Joseph. At the crown are the antiphonies of Advent, beginning with the «O». The arrangement of the windows, the contrast of light and shade in the chapels and, especially, the gargoyles and spires of the pinnacles, take their inspiration from the flora and fauna which grew around the very building: lizards, snails and sea-snails, salamanders, frogs and tadpoles.

The enlarged shoots of plants constitute an extraordinary naturalist vision at the service of architecture. Along the separating walls of the chapels, between the carved pedestal and baldachin are the founding saints Dominic, Anthony, Benedict, Elijah, Bruno, Francis, Clare, Bernard and Teresa.

Spikes inspired in the vegetation which surrounded the church.

The needles of the spires culminate in decorative spikes.

23

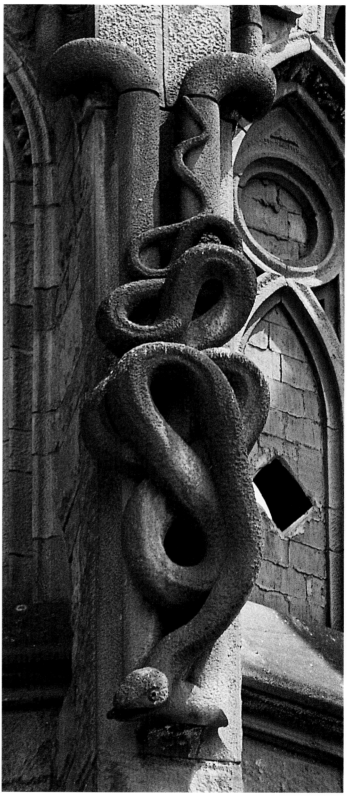

The gargoyles represent snails and snakes.

Apse spires.

4.- The cloister

The arrangement of the cloister, encircling the church, is very different from that of basilicas, monasteries or cathedrals. The cloister communicates portals, chapels and sacristies and, surrounding the church as it does, allows the circulation of processions whilst keeping out noise from the exterior. On the ground floor are lower spaces which can be used as workshops, services or storerooms.

Initially, Gaudí built the first two stretches on either side of the Façade of the Nativity, placing portals dedicated to Our Lady of the Rosary and of Montserrat in the irregular space between the bell-towers. These portals cover conical lanterns through which the daylight enters.

In order to show what could have been done, Gaudí completed the section dedicated to the Virgin of the Rosary with extraordinary craftsmanship. This is filigree work which reminds one of needlepoint or fine basket-weaving, adorned by roses and rosaries. The Virgin of the Rosary, with the Child, presides the archivolt of the portal, along with Saint Dominic and Saint Catherine of Siena. On either side of the portal are the Patriarchs, kings and prophets Isaac, Jacob, David and Solomon. In the corbels of the vault groins are representations of the Death of the Righteous One and the Temptations of Man and Woman. The text of the Ave Maria invites the faithful to make the angelic salutation, whilst the words «Et in hora mortis nostrae, Amen» give significance to the company of Jesus, Joseph and Mary as comfort to the dying. The temptations show the devil placing a bomb in the hands of a terrorist or with a purse with which he prostitutes women.

Floral and basketwork decoration in the cloister walls.

Rosary Portal.

Our Lady of the Rosary, Saint Dominic and Saint Catherine.

Play of light in the lantern of the Rosary Portal.

Angelic figures in the keystone of the first section of the cloister.

The temptation of man: violence.

5.- The façades

Gaudí proposed to built the Façade of the Nativity with the intention that his own generation should see it completed. This was a challenge to the continuation of the work, to the extent that future generations would have to terminate the parts of the church open to the public, increasing the time required for its construction.

Each of the three façades has three portals symbolising the theological virtues of Faith, Hope and Charity. They are crowned by four belltowers representing the Apostles. On these can be read the words Sanctus, Sanctus, Sanctus and Hosanna Excelsis. Gaudí wanted all, on reading this inscription, to praise the Lord.

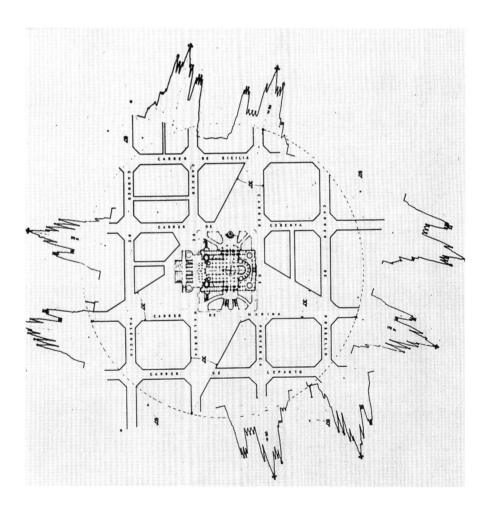

Silhouette of the church as Gaudí envisaged it, with the organisation of the church surroundings.

Aerial view of the church: Nativity Façade.

Aerial view of the church: apse.

Aerial view of the church: West and Passion Façades (June 1999).

a) Nativity Façade:

In the central archivolt, under the Star of the Orient, are Jesus, Mary and Joseph, between the ox and the mule, surrounded by singing angels. On either side are the Adoration of the Shepherds and the Magi. Higher up angels play trumpets announcing the Nativity, the Annunciation and the Coronation of Mary. Finally, there is a cypress tree, the refuge of birds, symbolising the Church as a huge spire crowned by a «Tau», the Greek initial letter designating the name of God. On the south side, around the Door of Hope, is the Wedding of Joseph and Mary, the Flight to Egypt, the Massacre of the Innocents, the nave of the Church steered by Joseph and, on the spire, the rock of Montserrat inscribed with the word «Sálvanos» («Save us»). On the other side is the Door of Faith, represented by the Visitation, Christ amongst the Doctors, the Presentation in the Temple and Jesus the Worker in his carpentry shop. In the spires are ears of wheat and grapes with the image of Mary in the dogma of the Immaculate.

Sculpture of the Holy Family by J. Busquets.

Nativity Façade: central doorway, or Portal of Charity.

Composition of stars completing a balcony.

Angels blowing bronze trumpets announce the birth of the Saviour.

Spire of the Portal of Hope: the Marriage of Joseph and Mary.

Spire of the Portal of Charity: the Coronation of Mary.

Portal of Hope.

Portal of Faith.

In the sills, domestic animals and floral motifs.

44

Spire of the Portal of Faith: the Immaculate.

b) Façade of the Passion:

Desolation, pain, sacrifice and death provide the counterpoint in the west front, which is presided over by the death of Christ so that his Resurrection and Ascension into Heaven can be proclaimed from the heights. The portal was planned in pain, after 1911, when Gaudí, ill in Puigcerdà had time on his hands to study and meditate on it. «I am ready», he said, «to sacrifice the building itself, to smash vaults and cut columns in order to give an idea of the cruelty of sacrifice».

The sculptor Josep Maria Subirachs created around 100 figures evoking the Passion of Christ, beginning with the figure of Christ on the Column in the mullion of the central portal.

Alone, the figure of Jesus bound is flanked on either side by the Betrayal of Judas and the Denial of Peter.

Above, the Via Dolorosa, with Jesus carrying the Cross after being condemned by Pilate. The figure of Veronica is at the centre, showing the image of the «Man of Pain», a face seen in negative, enveloped in mystery. Mary, Saint John, the Holy Women, the soldiers, the people... figures leading up to the scene of the Holy Sepulchre.

The image of Christ Resurrected ascending to Heaven, between the belltowers, will complete the representation of the human life of Christ in the catechistic vision of the Mystery of our Salvation.

Desolation and Pain at the death of Jesus Christ.

Passion Façade.

47

The Denial of Peter. The Centurion Longinus on horseback.

The Via Dolorosa and the death of Christ.

49

Jesus on the column and detail of the rope. The betrayal of Judas.

«Ecce Homo».

c) Façade of the Glory:

Gaudí left a study of the volumes and structure and of the iconographic and symbolic design of this main façade, which faces towards the sea. A monumental narthex gives way to three portals and is crowned by four belltowers flanked on either side by the Chapel of the Sacrament and the Baptistery. There are eleven doors leading directly or through the cloister into the chapels, and from these into the church itself. The central portal has three doors. The narthex is covered by the vaults under the belltower, hyperboloids and 15 lanterns. These are asymmetrical hyperboloids which cut and crown various cones. All is supported in view, on 21 columns, except for the connecting walls between the chapels and under the belltowers. The whole forms a large tympanum with ascending hyperboloids in which Gaudí envisioned an iconographic representation of the Glory.

Stony clouds are inscribed with the symbol of Faith, the Credo. The entrance, at the same level as the entire church, is high enough above Carrer Mallorca for this route to continue circulating below, and thus the narthex opens out into a great open space. On either side Gaudí imagined a 20 metre high waterspout and a huge flaming cresset purifying fire and water. The iconography presents man within the Order of Creation, his origin and his end, with the Way to achieve it. «Since Adam and Eve, through hard work and by practicing virtue, man can conquer the Glory Christ opened for us through Redemption and with the help of Grace». We also find here the Beatitudes, the Virtues and the capital sins: Hell is represented beneath the vaults of the street. Higher up is Purgatory and, over each of the seven entrance doors, representing the Sacraments, is a prayer to Our Father.

In the centre of the façade is Saint Joseph at work, with the attributes of the manual trades. Higher up, Mary presides as a Queen over the Saints, whilst at the top is Christ with the attributes of the Passion, with the seven trumpeting angels announcing the Last Judgement. The angel hierarchies surround the Eternal Father and, in the large central rose window, the Holy Spirit completes this vision of the Trinity.

Original model and study of volumes for the Glory Façade.

6.- The nave and aisles

The nave and aisles are made up of completely new forms with original geometric solutions and structures. They are the result of years of study and reflection. Gaudí began the project for the nave and aisles in around 1910, incorporating his experience with the chapel of the Colonia Güell. A solution with slightly helicoidal columns, arches and vaults, with hyperbolic paraboloids was published in 1917. The discovery of the luminous quality of hyperboloids led Gaudí to use them in the nave in a transept of concave-convex domes interweaving columns with walls and high windows. These forms, of which 1:10 models were made, form a vision of the forest which he often used as an image to explain his project. These columns, vaults, high windows and roofs form what Gaudí considered the final result of the design work, and the overall and structural lines of this definitive design were presented by his assistant, the architect Sugrañes in 1923 to the Catalan Association of Architects. This 1:10 scale model as designed by Gaudí is now being turned into reality. In it, forms are giving the continuity they are accorded in nature.

Side vaults. Original model by Gaudí.

Plaster model of the nave and aisles (1/10 scale).

a) The columns:

In itself, this new solution for vertical support conceived by Gaudí, leaning slightly «so as to follow the pressure curve supporting the weight of the roof» is an extraordinary creative innovation. From the intersection of two helicoids spring flutes, beginning at the concave sections of the starred polygon at the base and multiplying upward as they turn.

The first turn occurs at a height in metres equal to the number of sides in the polygon at the base. The second begins at a height in metres the same as half the number of sides in the same polygon, producing twice as many new flutes. The third turn, at a height one quarter of the number of metres of the same polygon, quadruples the number of flutes. In this way, then, at a height in metres double the number of sides at the base, the flutes have multiplied and the polygon has become circumference.

Gaudí's column is at once extraordinary and simple. It produces flutes which become finer and multiply as it rises, springing from the deepest parts of each flute. As it ascends, it combines both the lightness of helicoidal growth and the gravity of the Doric column.

This is a surprising, wholly new column of exceptional beauty. It will come as no surprise to learn that Gaudí planned to use it throughout the temple and with different polygons. The first was a starred octagon. In the naves and aisles, it springs from the hexagon, the square and the pentagon, the rectangle, the decahedron and the dodecahedron. Gaudí plays with them, inverts them, he «macles» them, achieving in architectural form the arboreal vision he gained from observing the trees outside his studio.

Restored original model of a capital, a convergence of ellipsoids (1/10 scale).

Arboreal vision of the columns.

Gaudí's workshop: original models of columns and vaults (1/10 scale).

Columns originally designed by Gaudí (May 1999).

Raising of columns and vaults in the side aisles.

The columns open up in branches to reach the vaults.

b) The vaults:

Over the lower columns, knots or capitals are the large elements which generate new columns which spring up like branches to the vaults. Their inclination follows the lines of pressure and reduces the light of the vaults. The intersection of the hyperboloids forming them are massive or empty, and are interwoven in starred forms. They form a tense, light whole which, as seen in the original 1:10 scale model, is in itself one of the achievements —though only in plaster— which best establish Gaudí's lasting contribution to 20th century architecture.

Gaudí planned these vaults to be rich in symbols and figures, with the anagrams of Jesus, Mary and Joseph in the central hyperboloids, and mosaics with angelic figures surrounding the figure of our Eternal Father at the rear of the apse, the central element in the mystical decoration of which Gaudí dreamed.

Nave vaults.

View of the vaults in the nave (1/10 scale plaster model).

Nave vaults (October 1999).

Detail of the Catalan vaults and continuation of the roofs.

c) The high windows:

The length of the nave and the transept are graceful windows allowing light to filter in through geometrical forms begun in the neo-Gothic side of the Façade of the Nativity, then changing into applications, though inscribed, of paraboloids, revolving and flat hyperboloids which, as Gaudí said, «make mouldings unnecessary, since light enters and is diffused in a play of varying intensity and colour». In the exterior, they are decorated with the fruits of each season, following the cycle of the year and symbolising fruits rained on all men and women by the Holy Spirit. In the mullion at the top of each window is a Founding Saint: Ignatius of Loyola, Vicente de Paúl, José de Calasanz, Felipe Neri, Pedro Nolasco, Antonio María Claret, Joaquina de Vedruna, Juan Bosco, etc.
Terminating each of these windows are baskets brimming with all kinds of fruit, representing the good works carried out.

High window in the side aisle, below the choir.

Lightened openwork walls of the high windows. Saint Vincent of Paúl and Saint Joseph of Calasanz (sculptors, N. Tortras and Cusachs).

Saint Joaquina of Vedruna (sculptor, Carulla).

Saint Vincent of Paúl (sculptor, N. Tortras).

Saint Antoni Maria Claret (sculptor, Domènec Fita).

View from the interior of a high window in the nave.

Terminals of the high windows, crowned by fruit-filled baskets.

Terminals of the high windows (sculptures by E. Sotoo).

d) The roofs:

These constitute one of the unique elements in the entire Sagrada Família, despite their functional purpose —intended as they are to protect the church from the rain and other elements. «A monumental unit of six domes lights the transept and the altar, exalting the entire church», said Gaudí, «culminating the pyramidisation of the building».

Over the last few years work on the church, Gaudí had completed the structural study of the building of which all we know are a number of sketches showing a similar structure to that of the sacristies, though longer, with an eight-pointed star cross-section rounded off by concave paraboloids Twelve and thirteen stories divide up the great height, with small columns and a sturdy double shell. On the outside is unfaced brick and stone. The dome of Our Lady covers the apse, which, due to its great width, appears as a cupola.

The roof of the nave is formed by pyramids —one per section— interconnected and with large paraboloids in the front of the windows. Small structures bearing the anagrams of the Holy Family support and crown lanterns 70 metres in height, with the words «Alleluia, Amen», on parabolic shields.

The space between the vaults and the roof is horizontally divided into four floors which support clusters of four small inclined columns which spring from the higher ramifications of the main columns. The aisles are covered by slightly sloping surfaces featuring beautifully resol-ved pyramid-shaped lanterns lighting the rafters and diffusing the light.

Weather-resistant stone from Montjuïc was proposed for the outer layer of the roof. With structural supports —floors and small columns, and the vaults making up the interior view— Gaudí's basic premise is ever-present: «Divide the inert loads and multiply the active elements».

Lantern for the side aisles. Original model, restored (1/10 scale).

Original model of the nave roof.

7.- Sacristies and chapels

«The paraboloid is the father of all geometry», Gaudí said. Consequently, he designed the double-faced cupola-like structures situated in the north and west corners of the cloister to feature an outstanding composition of these planes, leaving the angles covered by lanterns dedicated to the Ember days of Autumn and to the Advent. The cupola arris and the large parabolic spherical lunes of the extrados, of bare brick, are graceful and will be decorated with mosaics.

Gaudí made in-depth studies of the sacristies, which he also used to experiment with the construction of the domes dedicated to Jesus Christ and the Virgin Mary.

The Baptistery and the Chapel of the Sacrament occupy the corners of the main front. A rough sketch by Gaudí shows its structure supported by central columns and the enveloping penetration of the cloister. Externally similar to the sacristies, their corners also contain small chapels and lanterns dedicated to the Ember days of Lent and Pentecost.

First sections of the cloister of the Nativity Façade.

Plaster model of the sacristies (1/25 scale).

8.- The belltowers and domes

The first Belltower of Saint Barnabas first came into view on 30 November 1925. Gaudí expressed his delight at seeing how «That lance joined the heavens with the earth». The other three were completed by the architect Sugrañes, the master's successor and collaborator, who left the Nativity Façade almost complete. Twelve belltowers are included in the plans, reaching a height of from 98 to 112 metres over the floor of the church. In the Nativity Façade are Matthew, Judas, Simon and Barnabas, in that of the Passion, James, Bartholomew, Thomas and Philip, and in the Façade of the Glory are Andrew, Peter, Paul and James. The transept and apse are crowned with a further six domes dedicated to Jesus Christ, the Four Evangelists and Our Lady. The highest of these will be culminated by a 170 metre high cross. During the day, this will sparkle with mosaics, at night with spotlights which will be installed on it to illuminate the other belltowers and, from them, the whole city, in enactment of the words of Jesus, «I am the light» (John, 8, 12).

Gaudí worked long on the termination of the belltowers. In the model presented at the Paris Exhibition in 1910, the solution he planned was quite different: so-called «pineapple beacons» were to receive and project rays of symbolic light. Lack of resources, however, gave Gaudí more time to compose the geometrical figures symbolising the Apostles with the episcopal attributes, the ring, the mitre, the crosier and the cross. The almost 25 metre high terminations begin with letters proclaiming «Hosanna Excelsis» in an enveloping hexagonal ascending order, separating channels formed by dihedral angles decorated with pyramid-shaped encircling dark-green glazed baked brick.

Next, starred geometrical forms of gold and silver Venetian mosaics on a red background rise to converge at the confluence of the octahedron and a perforated sphere housing the reflectors and representing the episcopal ring. A triangular pyramid-shaped trunk curves round, forming the crosier, whilst two diverging curvilinear squares reveal the mitre as they mark out the cross.

The belltowers emerge from the mass of the three great portals in each façade, dedicated to the theological virtue. They have a double gallery in which ascend in the interior a helicoidal staircase, rising between the chiaroscuro of the ribs of vertical stone and the inclined planes ascending vertically. The inner space provides for the installation of the tubular bells Gaudí studied so that their chimes could be heard all around, accompanying celebrations.

Interior of a belltower.

The four belltowers on the east side.

The Apostle Barnaby in the belltower which bears his name.

The belltowers: architecture of stone and mosaic reaching to the sky.

9.- The schools

The parish schools were built in 1909 so as to begin implementing the provisional programme of the church. For this reason, the partly sunken floor of the aisles and a section of the cloisters is set aside for these schools. As Gaudí said: «by the side of the Church, the people will receive education and culture». The construction of a low-cost building adequate to fulfil this purpose was therefore undertaken on the large site available. In it, Gaudí demonstrated his enormous architectural capacity with surprising simplicity and complexity. Inside, inclined vertical partition walls support beams supporting and undulating roof, going from concave to convex in order to collect water and, at the same time, give greater structural resistance. The roofed span over the three classrooms was divided in half so that planks of standard length and section could be used. Standing wooden beams and a crossbeam running the length of the building divide the rectangle around the perimeter.

A fire started by revolutionary extremists in July 1936 destroyed the schools, which were later rebuilt by the architect Quintana with a number of modifications to the original plans. In due course, they will be rebuilt according to the original plans.

Period photograph of a schoolroom.

View of the Church Schools.

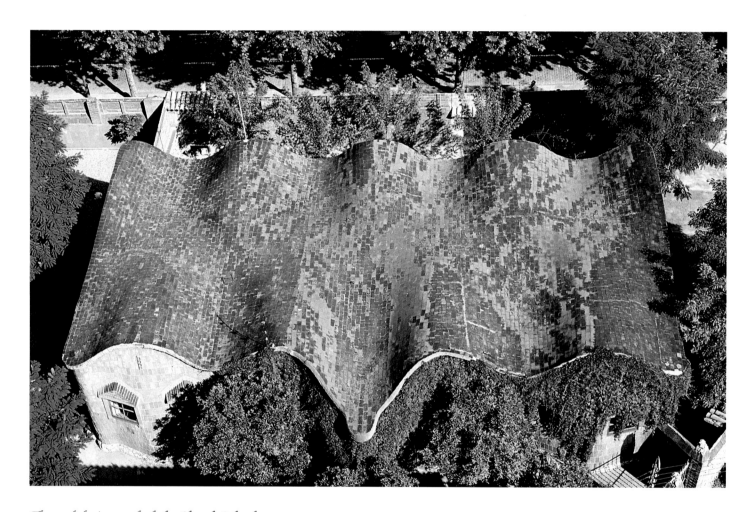

The undulating roof of the Church Schools.

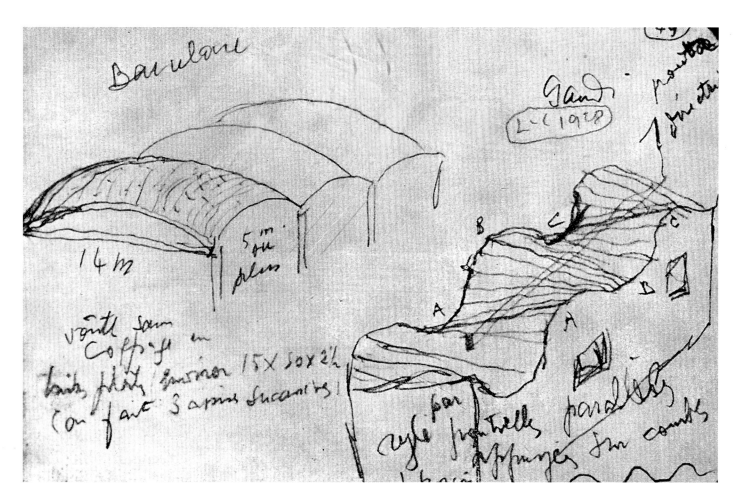

Sketch made by Le Corbusier during his visit to the church.

THE STRUCTURE

Gaudí drew up his first plans for the church based on the Gothic style. He stressed the verticality of the elements, as can be appreciated in his sketch of the entire building seen from the apse («El Propagador», 1891).

The extraordinary and intelligent solution of raising the Nativity Façade with the possibilities this afforded of obtaining a large donation prolonged the time required to draw up the overall plan for the church. The economic precariousness of the project was, in fact, a help, contributing to the fact that Gaudí devoted the last twelve years of his life to making the Sagrada Familia the most important architectural feat of the 20th century, structurally speaking. In the search for pressure curves and the desire for them to coincide with the architectural forms, he decided to incline the columns, identifying the mechanical and architectural organism in each element. In this way, he ramified the columns from a given height upwards to divide the dead weights of the vaults by multiplying the active resistant elements. The result is an arboreal, balanced, light structure which considerably reduces the great construction masses required by a Gothic cathedral. Moreover, Gaudí planned to use reinforced concrete to reduce the scaffolding needed to support the weight of the building until it could be balanced.

Furthermore, Gaudí selected the most resistant natural materials capable of supporting the heavy loads supported by the other domes and stone roofs planned which, at the same time, fireproofed the building, their loads also helping to absorb seismic tremors.

Now, using computers, the feasibility of Gaudí's original project has been fully demonstrated.

Model of the inverted study Gaudí made to calculate the proportions and design the Chapel of the Colònia Güell.

Drawing of the church made by Joan Rubio following Gaudí's instructions.

Longitudinal section of the building. Study carried out under the direction of Puig Boada and Bonet Garí.

GEOMETRICAL MODELLING

Gaudí was fully aware that he would never see the completion of the church his creative genius dreamed of. He had very clear ideas about the synthesis of structure and form he wanted to achieve, however. Thanks to his knowledge of curved forms generated by a straight line, that is, ruled surfaces —the hyperbolic paraboloid, the helicoid, the hyperboloid and the conoid— and their structural and plastic possibilities regarding lighting, and of sound, and all the beauty he had observed in nature, led him to leave them volumetrically resolved, making them clearly defined and easily to apply in the future.

Over the last twelve years of his life, devoted exclusively to the Sagrada Familia, Gaudí studied and produced a series of 1/10 scale plaster models which culminated his contribution to architecture.

All the plans were burnt when Gaudí's studio was sacked by revolutionaries in 1936, but the plaster models, though broken, survived the destruction. Close study of them revealed the geometrical modelling Gaudí wished to establish so that the work he planned could be continued according to his design. These are simple proportions repeated throughout the Sagrada Familia, based on multiples and divisions of twelve, commonly used in Catalonia since the Middle Ages. The intercolumn of 7.5 metres, repeated twelve times, gives the 90 metres of the length of the interior of the church, producing the following series:

90 - 82,5 - 75 - 67,5 - 60 - 52,5 - 45 - 37,5 - 30 - 22,5 - 15 - 7,5
12   11   10   9   8   7   6   5   4   3   2   1

This is one of the many mathematical series forming the measurements of the church which, taken together, weave the immense network which models it geometrically. The convergence of structure and form through geometry allows us to obtain the same results Gaudí had obtained and, of course, many of those he did not materially resolve, thanks to the geometrical modelling he conceived.

Models of the church as they were displayed during the time of Gaudí.

SYMBOLISM

«The entire Church of the Sagrada Familia is a hymn of praise to God intoned by Humanity and of which each stone is a verse sung in a clear, powerful, harmonious voice», writes Puig Boada. It was clear to Gaudí that this was to be the church of the people, a song to the Trinity of God.

In its exterior, the Sagrada Familia building symbolises the Church, Jesus Christ and the faithful, represented by Mary, the Apostles and the Saints. The twelve belltowers represent the Apostles, the first bishops of the Church, the voice which exhorts the faithful, great witnesses to the revelation received. Inside, the columns supporting the vaults and roof also represent the Apostles and the local churches with their saints, that is to say, everyone, from the Catalan dioceses to those of the five continents, as well as celestial Jerusalem, the mystical city of peace the Lamb of God has won for us.

Gaudí said that the nave and aisles and the vaults would be «Like a forest. Light will enter in abundance through windows placed at different heights. It will be possible to follow the main daily prayers (the Te Deum, the Miserere, the Benedictus and the Magnificat) from the inscriptions on the handrails of the choir and the triforiums». Outstanding of the columns encircling the transept and apse, dedicated to the Apostles and the Evangelists, are those of the Apostles Peter and Paul, which join the triumphal arch with the Calvary, the Virgin Mary, the Crucifixion and Saint John. The representation of the Trinity will be completed by the image of the Eternal Father which will be seen by entering the church in the dome of the apse with a seven-armed lamp, symbolising the Holy Spirit. The inscription of the Hymn of Glory and the hanging canopy which protects the altar, will centre the attention of worshippers here. In the triforium on the side of the Façade of the Passion is the Virgin Mary, surrounded by angels with the attributes of the Litanies. In that of the Nativity is Saint Joseph with the attributes of his trade, completing, along with the crucifix at the altar, the representation of the Holy Family.

«Sursum Corda» («Lift up the hearts»), inscribed mid-way up the belltowers.

The sow represents Joseph, the flutes form the initial letter of Mary's name and the cross above symbolises Jesus.

Detail of the candelabrum for the tenebrae: the sword traversing Mary; Alpha and Omega.

Nativity Portal: decorative composition with rosaries.

Charity Portal: a cypress (the Church) in which birds (the faithful) find shelter.

The Annunciation and, in the ogees, signs of the Zodiac.

PLASTICITY

For any work of architecture to be considered beautiful, its elements must have be appropriately located and be fitting in size, shape and colour.

a) Nature.

Gaudí's plasticity is based on his study of nature, and is expressed in forms and colours. As mentioned previously, Gaudí commented on his learning from nature as follows: «This tree, next to my workshop, is my master». Observing it, he drew conclusions which he put into practice in his projects. The use of natural forms, of flora and fauna, is frequent throughout his work and in many of the details of the Church of the Sagrada Familia. Abstract geometrical forms are derived from the study of nature, the result of combinations of convergences and new forms which had never before been used in architecture.

Snail gargoyle in the apse.

Tortoise which serves as the base of a column in the Nativity Façade.

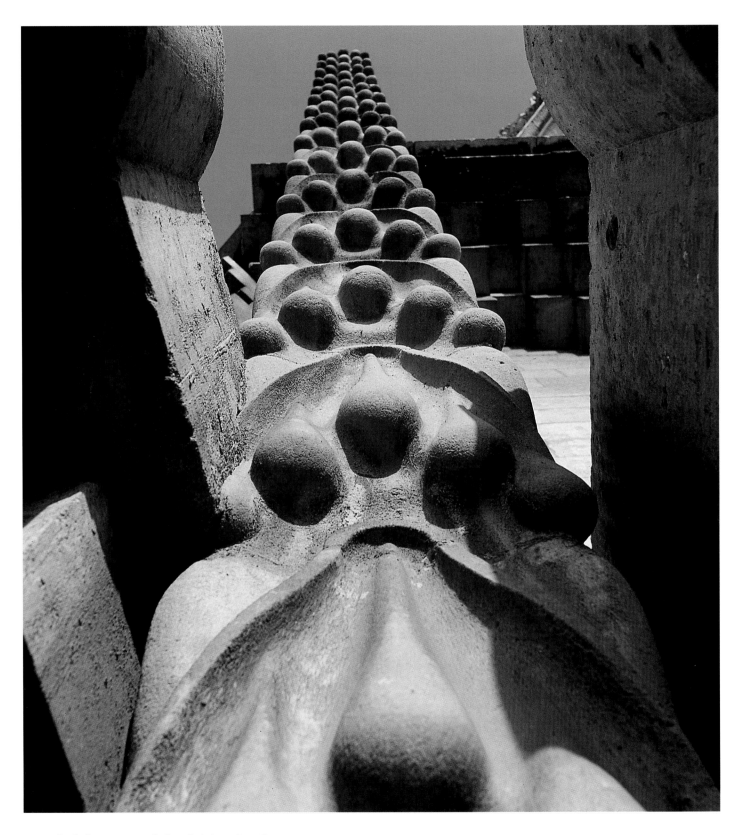

Detail of the interior of the Nativity Façade.

Spiral staircase inspired in natural forms.

b) Form.

Natural forms are present even in the capitals in the crypt and the gargoyles and spires of the apse. In the Nativity Façade, the human figure, plants and animals are present, expressing the Mystery of the Nativity, with all that which surrounds the childhood of Jesus. They are also found in the windows, in the sculptural motifs representing fruits from the different seasons of the year. Geometrical forms based on simple elements and drawings became more complicated as the study and use of curved surfaces became more familiar to Gaudí. He first made use of paraboloids, then hyperboloids, producing a great range of theoretic and formal innovation. The columns, windows and vaults Gaudí planned in the later years of his life are the exponent of an extraordinary work of research and study. This is also true of the belltowers, the domes and other elements.

Wrought-iron torch-holder.

Detail of the Rosary Portal in the cloister.

103

Frame and closure of one of the grilles.

Inner console of the Nativity Façade.

c) Colour.

Colour is another important element in Gaudí's architecture. In the Church of the Sagrada Familia, the terminations of the belltowers are the finest exponent of the results obtained from his use of colour. A model demonstrating Gaudí's ideas for the Nativity Façade in a scale of 1/25 was made for the Paris Exhibition in 1910, but was, unfortunately, destroyed in 1936. From it however, some of Gaudí's theories were applied in the chapel in the Colonia Güell and other works.

Gaudí planned to use Venetian mosaic, which would make the colour lasting, a sign of life, not ephemeral like ceramic mosaic.

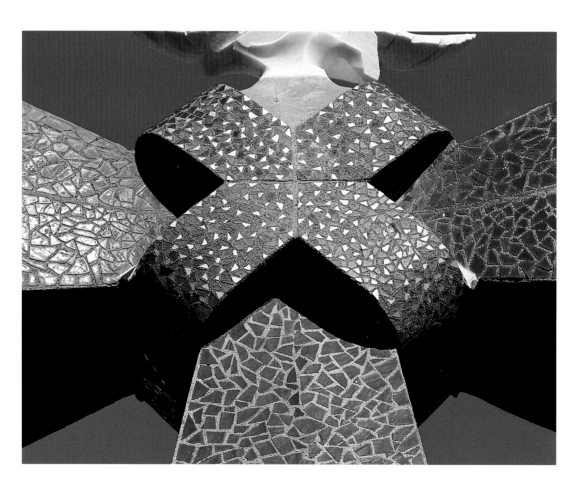

Detail of the cypress forming the terminal of the Nativity Façade.

Terminals of the belltowers with the Episcopal symbols: the cross, the ring, the mitre and the crosier.

Detail of the boss of a Venetian mosaic.

Terminal of a belltower: Venetian mosaic and paving stones.

Flèche of the spire over a high window.

110

Stained-glass window in the crypt.

111

d) Acoustics and lighting.

Gaudí had studied acoustic problems and experimented with the tubular bells he installed in the elongated hollowed sections of the belltowers, as well as with the organs which were to fill the naves with resounding music. There are singers' galleries on either side of the nave, in the interior of the rear section of the Façade of the Glory and over the ambulatory in the apse, where there is space for the children's choir, with total capacity for 1,500 choristers. With the priests around the altar, Gaudí felt certain that the people would take part in services, showing himself, as in many other questions, to anticipate the II Vatican Council's decisions regarding the liturgy. Light, entering harmoniously through the great high windows, diffused by the new geometrical surfaces, will prevent excessive contrasts, giving greater visibility to the decorated surfaces. Spotlights placed at the mouths of the hyperboloids of the vaults add diffused lighting at night, accompanied by that from the stained glass windows, leaded in accordance with the new procedure tried out in Majorca Cathedral, will accompany with maximum brilliance of the polychrome glass the stained-glass window, made without paint or enamel. As Gaudí explained, «The church will be full of light, with beautiful filtering effects, combining that coming in from the domes with that from the glass of the glazed high windows. All this will illuminate the polychrome of the interior».

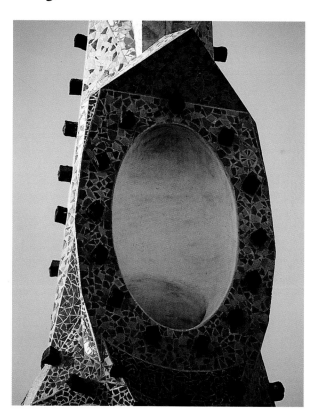

Space in the belltowers for the installation of reflectors.

The belltowers were designed for the external projection of music and lighting.

113

Sounding boards in the belltowers to relay music to the exterior.

Night-time illumination of the Nativity Façade.

e) Liturgical objects.

Gaudí planned the altars, objects and furnishings for worship in the church, giving us liturgical instruction through the dignity and quality of each item: the benches, the sacristy cupboards, the pulpit and the confessional boxes, the candelabras and the credence tables, the seats for the officiants, the lamps and the chandeliers. Particularly outstanding are the candlestand and the lectern. Gaudí himself had a personal hand in making some of these pieces.

Paschal candle.

Portable pulpit.

Candelabrum for the tenebrae services at Easter, and cross with candelabrum.

Detail of a lectern.

PRESENT STATE AND IMMEDIATE FUTURE

Today, little over half the building can be considered complete: the crypt, the Nativity and Passion façades (the pediment and high window have still to be completed in this front) and the walls enclosing the apse, up to the spires. The vaults over the nave and aisles are complete, and work continues on those of the transept and the crossing columns. Overall an area of 1,500 square metres of vaults over nave, aisles and transept.

The faithful and the friends of the Church of the Sagrada Familia are the spiritual support which keeps this idea in constant movement forward, and work continues thanks to the donations, large and small, which are received daily. To this must be added the selfless dedication of the many people working on the project: technicians, masons, sculptors, stone-cutters, mechanics, carpenters, etc.

The administration is austere, making it possible to adapt the rhythm of the work to that at which income is received in the form of donations of all types.

Technically, the aim is for the most modern technology to be employed: computers to calculate the structure or work the stone, together with quality control of the stone and concrete used, or the new machinery and technologies created to improve the work rate and safety of construction. A new 140-metre crane installed over the upper floor of the nave vaults allows heavier pieces to be raised both more easily and more quickly, its 60-metre arm allowing the apse and the domes of the evangelists to be closed.

Many ask, «When will it be finished?» This is a difficult question to answer, as it depends on the donations received, but there is a programme for the immediate present and another for the near future which gradually put into effect the proposals of the Foundation's Board of Trustees. Gaudí took from 40 to 50 years to build just one façade along with the crypt and the walls of the apse. Then came the upheaval of the Spanish Civil War, which saw the work paralysed for some 20 years. The generation of those who knew Gaudí —his direct followers— took another 20 years to complete the Façade of the Passion. The challenge now is to terminate the vaults by the beginning of the 21st century, but even then there will still be much to do: the domes of the crossing and apse have to be raised, the roofs and the Façade of the Glory built, and all those elements Gaudí left in the form of precise ideas, like a dream of the future, made reality.

Work on the closure of the transept vaults (May 1999)

Crane installed on the upper floor of the nave.

Work in the interior of the church (May 1999).

Chronology of the Church of the Sagrada Familia:

1886   Josep Maria Bocabella founds the «Associació de Devots de Sant Josep» (Association of Followers of Saint Joseph), which would become the promoter of the Church of the Sagrada Familia.

1882   First stone laid. Project by architect Villar.

1883   Antoni Gaudí becomes the architect of the church.

1889   The crypt is finished.

1890   Drawing of the first overall solution.

1892   Work begins on Nativity Façade.

1894   Apse front completed.

1899   Completion of the Portal of the Rosary in the cloister.

1909   Building of the parish school.

1910   Exhibition in Paris of the model of the Nativity Façade.

1917   Project for the Façade of the Passion, with the monument to Bishop Torres i Bages.

1923   Final solution for nave, aisles and roofs in 1:10 and 1:25 scale plaster models.

1925   30 November. First belltower (Saint Barnabas), 100 metres high, finished.

1926   Antoni Gaudí dies in an accident on 10 June.

1930   The four belltowers of the Nativity Façade completed.

1936   Spanish Civil War. Profanation and destruction in the church. Gaudí's studio destroyed.

1940   Restoration of the crypt and plaster models.

1954   Work begins on the Façade of the Passion.

1977   The four belltowers of the Façade of the Passion completed.

1978   Work begins on the fronts of the nave and aisles.

1986-90 Foundations of the nave and aisles. First sculptures for the Façade of the Passion.

1995   Construction of the aisle vaults.

1997   Construction of the nave.

1998   Construction of the nave.

2000   Closing of the vaults over the transept and crossing.

Antoni Gaudí at the Corpus Christi procession. Barcelona Cathedral, 1924.

EPILOGUE

Whether or not the work of building the Temple Expiatori de la Sagrada Família continues depends, fundamentally, on the public will. A few years ago, before the nave and aisles began to be built, Cardinal Jubany, Archbishop of Barcelona, took the decision that it should be so because the will of the people was being expressed in the constant contribution of donations, mostly small amounts, but many in number, accompanied from time to time by larger gifts or legacies.

Why do people ask insistently the question «When will the Sagrada Família be finished?» Gaudí himself was asked this question, and he replied «My client is in no hurry». Why does the monument receive so many visitors? It is difficult to answer this question, but the construction of this church, dedicated to Jesus, Mary and Joseph, the Holy Family of Nazareth, is the expression of solidarity, of Faith and Hope embraced by Love which, with its invocation of God the Father, our Creator, is the sign of the brotherhood of all human beings.

CONTENTS